]

52 Ways To Inform Coworkers They're Stupid

Published by Upgraded Books

Copyright © 2024 Upgraded Books

Also by Upgraded Books

- *Ways To Make Your Co-Workers Feel Awkward*
- *HR Approved Way To Say Things I Can't Say Out Loud At Work*
- *HR Approved Ways To Look Smart At Work*
- *Brilliant Ideas I Had While Taking A Dump*

Download Your Free Guide

Email Like A Pro Cheat Sheet: *HR Approved Ways of Emailing Your Stupid Coworkers*

https://bit.ly/465COao

HR NOTE

Dear Valued Employee,
Karen from HR here. I understand
that, from time to time, we all need
ways to let off some steam,
especially when dealing with
coworkers who are... not necessarily
the brightest. This, conveniently, is
also great for company morale. So,
in that spirit, enjoy this book! P.S.
Look out for little notes from me
scattered here and there.

HR MEMO

HR confirms that idiocy, while challenging to deal with, is not an official allergen. In any case, attempting to reduce exposure is understandable.

I'd love to stay and chitchat, but I'm allergic to idiots

As per my last
email...

HR MEMO

While HR is always supportive of continuous learning, we must remind employees that education is a journey, not a final destination. Some just have a bit more distance to cover.

This one has been untouched by knowledge or education

Dense as a
bowling bowl,
nowhere near as
useful

You're smarter than you look

Did you happen to be accidentally dropped on the head as a baby?

It would explain a lot

You certainly have your own... uh... let's call it unique perspectives

I feel right now
like you're an
absolute moron.

I'm asking you to
please respect
that feeling.

HR MEMO

We strive for the utmost professionalism here at our company. This includes avoiding a circus-like atmosphere in the office. So yes, let's leave the clown shoes at home.

If I said I agree with you, we'd both be f*cking clowns now, wouldn't we?

APPROVED

So let's not turn this into a circus

Not the sharpest tool in the company shed, now are we?

My face always contorts this way... not only when you're spewing stupidity

Your mouth is open and there's noise coming out. You might want to look into that

I thought we APPROVED already established that you're not to walk around the office with scissors?

Every time you open your mouth, I'm like WTF. And I'm not talking about just your breath.

APPROVED

HR MEMO

HR believes in the value of diverse teams, though we encourage you to avoid comparing your colleagues to muppets, even though it may be a warranted comparison.

I guess every company has its muppets

Your talent is in demand at the moment. I heard the circus is short a few clowns?

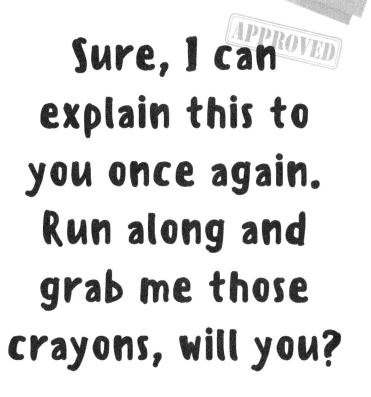

Sure, I can explain this to you once again. Run along and grab me those crayons, will you?

Sarcasm is my body's natural defense mechanism against stupidity

Bless Your Heart

HR MEMO

HR fully supports your need to adjust your glasses. Having said that, we encourage the use of your index finger to avoid any accidental misinterpretation.

(Adjust your reading glass rim with the middle finger)

Keep talking.
Maybe you'll
eventually say
something not so
f*cking stupid

Yeah keep rolling
your eyes...
maybe you'll find
something useful
back there

I don't need to imply that you're an absolute spoon... your words are doing all the work for you!

HR MEMO

HR encourages patience but we also understand that there are limits to how much stupidity any single human being can tolerate.

My ability to handle your stupidity is diminishing with each word you say

APPROVED

I bear no APPROVED
responsibility for
what my face
does when you
talk. With that
said, you can now
start talking.

Look here, we've got dumb and dumber to grace us with their presence in the meeting today. Welcome. Here's some glue.

APPROVED

AWESOME Input.

Anyway...

I'm may not be a PhD, but I definitely know a muppet when I see one

Someone wise once said, 'Don't be an idiot.' You've clearly missed that memo.

HR MEMO

HR appreciates employee
curiosity about safety
labels although perhaps
such realizations could
remain more of a
personal reflection.

I've always wondered who they made those 'Contents Hot' warning labels on coffee cups for.

Now it all makes sense.

Before you open your mouth, I know what you're going to say: "I'm a dumbass"

Please stop talking immediately.

I can tell that my brain cells are committing suicide.

APPROVED

The issue isn't with the computer — it stems from the moron matter in between the keyboard and the chair

Sure, I'd love to
help you out.

Which way did
you come in?

HR MEMO

HR supports taking breaks when conversations turn unproductive, however, we recommend using a more positive approach when taking a pause such as "Let's revisit this once we've had time to reflect"

Let's hit pause on this dumpster fire of a conversation for now

I'm not being a smartass. I'm a trained professional in pointing out the ridiculously obvious

HR MEMO

We discourage references to any particularly unsanitary habits in workplace communication. More constructive, professional feedback is recommended.

Have you been licking the bus windows again?

By the way, your contribution in today's meeting. Clap clap. You're the human embodiment of a participation award.

There doesn't
seem to be
anything
happening
upstairs

Your presence here is like that one time I burned my hand on the grill — unnecessary and painful

You've set a low bar for yourself yet you still manage to miss the bar altogether

It's better to keep them guessing than to open your mouth and remove all doubt

As mentioned
during our
meeting...

HR MEMO

HR would generally prefer it if you chose a game that fosters team collaboration.

APPROVED

Let's play a game
of f*ck off...

You start

Sorry, did the middle of my sentence interrupt the beginning of yours?

Stop lingering around there like a stray fart

Did you come up
with that all by
your pretty
little self?

It must be nice
not being tied
down by thought
processes

Let's all be radically honest here and realize that I'm not insulting you — I'm describing you

HR MEMO

HR suggests engaging with colleagues under the assumption that someone's home — even when it really doesn't seem that way.

It looks like the light's on but nobody's there

(Dial up the volume on your smartphone playing music while the other person is still talking)

It's not possible
for me to think
any less of you

Thank you for reading this book!

I hope I got at least one laugh out of you :)

I would be incredibly grateful if you could take just 30 seconds to leave me a review! Reviews are crucial for an author's livelihood and surprisingly difficult to come by.

The more reviews my books receive, the more I can continue pursuing my love for creating books. If you have any thoughts about this book, please leave a review and let me know.

- Sam

Printed in Great Britain
by Amazon

55575357R00066